Homesteading Ideas for Growing What You Eat In Your Garden

No BS Guide on Homesteading and Self Sufficiency

William Whittaker

I dedicate this book to Brittany, who introduced me to homesteading. My life has not been the same since.

Copyright © 2014 by Speedy Publishing LLC

All rights reserved. No part of this publication may be reproduced, distributed or transmitted in any form or by any means, including photocopying, recording, or other electronic or mechanical methods, without the prior written permission of the publisher, except in the case of brief quotations embodied in critical reviews and certain other noncommercial uses permitted by copyright law. For permission requests, write to the publisher, addressed "Attention: Permissions Coordinator," at the address below.

Speedy Publishing LLC (c) 2014
40 E. Main St., #1156
Newark, DE 19711
www.speedypublishing.co

Ordering Information:
Quantity sales; Special discounts are available on quantity purchases by corporations, associations, and others. For details, contact the "Special Sales Department" at the address above.

-- 1st edition

Manufactured in the United States of America

TABLE OF CONTENTS

PUBLISHER'S NOTES.. i

CHAPTER 1: HOMESTEADING 1

CHAPTER 2: HOW TO SET UP YOUR VEGETABLE GARDEN 3

CHAPTER 3: HOW TO IMPROVE THE SOIL.. 7

CHAPTER 4: HOW TO PLANT VEGETABLES AND FRUITS 10

CHAPTER 5: HOW TO SET UP GARDEN IRRIGATION.................................. 12

CHAPTER 6: HOW TO KEEP YOUR GARDEN PEST FREE............................. 16

CHAPTER 7: WHAT CROPS TO PLANT IN YOUR GARDEN 21

MEET THE AUTHOR 27

Publisher's Notes

Disclaimer

This publication is intended to provide helpful and informative material. It is not intended to diagnose, treat, cure, or prevent any health problem or condition, nor is intended to replace the advice of a physician. No action should be taken solely on the contents of this book. Always consult your physician or qualified health-care professional on any matters regarding your health and before adopting any suggestions in this book or drawing inferences from it.

The author and publisher specifically disclaim all responsibility for any liability, loss or risk, personal or otherwise, which is incurred as a consequence, directly or indirectly, from the use or application of any contents of this book.

Any and all product names referenced within this book are the trademarks of their respective owners. None of these owners have sponsored, authorized, endorsed, or approved this book.

Always read all information provided by the manufacturers' product labels before using their products. The author and publisher are not responsible for claims made by manufacturers.

Print Edition 2014

CHAPTER 1: HOMESTEADING

Anyone who is interested in living a frugal lifestyle can learn a lot from homesteaders. What exactly is homesteading, and how can these practices be integrated with the frugal lifestyle?

While the term homesteading refers to any individual who opts to get back to basics and live a more self-sustaining lifestyle there are actually three different types. First, there is the homesteader who is not even on the grid. Off-the-grid individuals live off the land and provide for their families by growing, raising, trading and making what they need. Other types of homesteaders do use some homesteading methods, but they are not completely dependent on livestock and the land to attain everything that they require.

Homesteaders produce most of what they need on their own.

The perfect example of this lifestyle is the Amish. I live pretty close to an Amish community. I am always in awe of how they get things done.

They keep certain practices alive, like canning preserves or even hanging laundry. Think about it - when was the last time you hand washed any clothing or hung your laundry out to dry?

Urban homesteading has recently become more popular as a result of the economy, along with changes in our awareness of what we eat. People who live a thrifty lifestyle already put into practice some of the aspects of urban homesteading without even knowing it.

Urban homesteading includes some form of agriculture (not on a large scale) in a city or urban setting. The practice of baking your own bread or growing your own tomatoes is an example. Growing herbs is also considered part of homesteading.

You can use as many homesteading practices as you like. Even in the city, with a permit you can own a few chickens if you have the space (and the neighbors don't mind). Nothing beats fresh eggs.

Chapter 2: How To Set Up Your Vegetable Garden

When putting a plan together for a vegetable garden, it is not hard to jump in headfirst and attempt to grow everything in the first year. A lot of experienced gardeners will advise that this is not the best thing to do - as you are basically setting yourself up for disappointment if you try. There is a lot to learn about care and maintenance - in no time you may have more weeds that anything in your garden.

Make a list of the vegetables that you like to eat. Then narrow the list down to those that are best consumed fresh or those that are just too expensive to purchase on a regular basis.

After your list is done, create a plan to build a couple of vegetable beds yearly, expanding as you learn and become more confident. Using weed suppressant fabric or woodchips to create clear paths makes a huge difference in the quality of your garden and will cut down on maintenance costs.

If the space that you are going to use for your garden is new, then you need to decide the type of garden you want as well as the system of planting that you want to utilize. There are several options, like square foot gardening, traditional rows, raised beds, etc. You should have garden beds that are approximately 4 feet wide (1.2 meters) and have a 2 foot path (60 centimeters) between them. They can be as long as you like, with space permitting - any wider and it will be a bit difficult to get to the middle of the bed without having to step on the soil in the bed itself. If there are children in your household, it is better to have raised beds with clearly marked edges.

Companion Planting

A variety of crop layouts can work in a specific garden space, which will allow for more variety in what is harvested. Experienced gardeners often have intricate planting systems that they swear by.

They may mix plants to deter pests (if there is a large area with a single crop, it is a beacon calling to them).

Cauliflower, broccoli and cabbages need protection from caterpillars and can be grown together, so they can be placed under horticultural fleece or a tunnel of netting.

Plants that attract helpful insects can also be grown. There are a few well-known types of flowers that serve to attract "good" insects like hoverflies, ladybugs and ladybirds, which are natural forms of pest control.

Support and shade also has to be considered - taller plants can be used to provide support for other plants like climbing beans which can be grown on sweet corn, or can simply provide shade.

Here are recommendations on how to place your plants in your vegetable garden:

Tender Plants

Plants like basil, eggplant, peppers and tomatoes require a lot of care. If you live in a climate that is extremely warm they can be planted anywhere, but if not, the sunniest spots in your garden are best for these crops. Walls that are south-facing work well, as they will get the heat necessary to produce a bumper crop.

Roaming Plants

After sorting out the tender plants, you can move on to what are known as roaming plants. These plants produce vines that go all over the garden like squash and melons. These need to be placed on the edge of the garden beds to prevent their large leaves from covering the other plants. They will also get more room to spread.

Vertically Climbing Plants

This group has to be planted where they will not shade the other vegetables. This group includes cucumbers, some types of squash and peas. Spinach and lettuce can do with the shade if you live in an exceptionally hot climate.

Irrigation

Strawberries, onions and celery do not thrive in dry weather conditions. Lower areas of your garden work better because they tend to have more moisture, though some form of irrigation should be considered to get the best crops if dry weather is an issue.

Pollination

Some plants need to be close to others to pollinate successfully and make fruit. One such crop is sweet corn, which is best grown in blocks to guarantee that the cobs are full.

Accessibility

You need to know which crops you want to harvest on a regular basis, be it herbs, tomatoes or cabbage. They should be as close to the kitchen as possible. You will need easy access to get rid of slugs and weeds more regularly.

Succession Planting

If you have limited space or want to grow a crop throughout the season, think about making use of intercropping or succession planting.

Don't Overcrowd

Last but not least, though it may be a tempting thought, take great care not to overcrowd plants while you go about completing your plan. This is the major mistake that new gardeners tend to make which is why plants tend to look small when they are seedlings.

Is it a Science or an Art?

Gardening is both a science and an art, which tends to confuse a lot of novice gardeners. There are a number of scientific principles to be followed. Poor quality soil and overcrowding in your garden will lead to little or no yield. In addition to that, the need to rotate crops later on will add more challenges.

The art of gardening comes in with deciding how the plants are to be placed to maximize the use of space without ignoring the rules.

Chapter 3: How To Improve The Soil

If the soil you have is less than perfect, you need some organic matter. This works well when you want to improve sandy or clay soil. You will not be able to change the type of soil you have, but when you add organic matter it will make it more like loam, which is great for the roots of plants. Even if you have loamy soil, plant matter should be added each year.

Organic matter helps to revamp garden soil in the following ways:

- It works to aerate and loosen clay soil.
- It improves the capability of sandy soil to retain nutrients and water.
- It supplies the material that attracts worms, beneficial fungi, microorganisms and other organisms that improve the health of vegetables.

Mix Organic Matter Into Soil

Before you start planting for the season, mix some organic matter into the soil. If you have raw organic matter like manure and leaves, it should be mixed with the soil at least a month before any planting takes place.

This will allow the components to break down before you plant. Also add some more finished manure and compost before you begin.

The following steps should be taken to properly add organic matter to soil:

- One or two inches of organic matter should be added to the area that you plan to use for planting.
- If the garden soil is very sandy, has heavy clay or is new, add two inches of organic matter. If the plot is not new or has loamy soil, one inch can be used.
- You will also need approximately three cubic yards of compost to place over one thousand square feet.
- The organic matter should be mixed to at least a depth of six inches.

Of course there is nothing great about spreading manure. The best way to get it done is to use a wheelbarrow and a shovel. The soil can be turned over with a rototiller, iron fork, or shovel.

Making Use of Compost

Compost is the recommended organic material. The process of composting breaks down sludge, wood scraps, agricultural waste and yard waste into humus. Humus is a crumbly material.

Compost is easy to use, and it is clean and readily available. It can be purchased by the truckload or in bags, depending on how much you need. A lot of sites that are assigned for waste disposal also make compost, and it does not cost much to purchase. If you need to save money, you can always make your own.

Before you purchase compost, find out if the compost contains any heavy metals like lead, and whether or not it is safe to place on a vegetable garden. The people working at your local waste disposal company should be able to tell you the nutrient content if they have done the necessary tests.

Using Manure and Sawdust

Making use of other materials like manure and sawdust can work as well but they pose some challenges that compost does not.

Sawdust is a way to add organic matter to soil and it will break down into humus but it tends to reduce the level of nitrogen in the soil as soon as it decomposes, so more fertilizer has to be added to make up for the loss.

Manure from livestock helps to improve the nitrogen level in the soil but bear in mind that the diet of livestock is made up of hay that tends to be full of weed seeds, which will then grow in a vegetable garden.

A lot of manure, like horse manure, will add nutrients and organic matter to the soil, but it also contains a lot of bedding materials like hay that can rob the soil of nitrogen as it breaks down.

If you do use manure, ensure that it has been around for a year or more to make sure that it is properly decomposed and that all the salts are out. If there is too much salt in the soil it can be harmful to plants. Better manure will have an earthy smell and will be dark brown in color.

Chapter 4: How To Plant Vegetables And Fruits

To be able to plant and harvest a great vegetable crop, you do not need to have a degree in horticulture or even a green thumb. It may seem an intimidating task, but it can be done once you are aware of a few tip and tricks. Once you truly know how, growing vegetables is much easier and a lot more enjoyable.

Making Selections

This is the most essential part of the process, especially for beginners. Select plants that are easy to plant and maintain, like potatoes or tomatoes. Squash also works well. These plants do not require a lot of attention. They only need to be watered regularly, and to have fertilizer added and weeds removed as needed.

They are also pretty easy to harvest as they can be picked quickly by hand. You can always find out which vegetables to plant in your area by going to garden seminars (if they are held) or by checking gardening publications.

Planning the Dates for Planting

When it comes to vegetable gardening it is essential to stick to the planting date. Vegetables are to be planted within a specific timeframe based on the location of the garden. These dates can be found online. Dates will be partially dependent on whether the planting will be indoors or outdoors. Indoor planting can be done at any time. Outdoor planting, obviously, is a bit more specific.

Conditions for Planting

A certain number of conditions need to be in place for planting. Based on the type of vegetable that is to be planted, shade/sun preference needs to be considered, along with planting depth and plant spacing. Plant spacing is extremely important as it gives the plant to necessary space that it needs to grow to maturity. Potatoes and tomatoes grow a lot of foliage and need room.

Overcrowding can occur if vegetables are planted too close together and it will decrease the yield. Vegetables also have to be planted at the right depth to enable the roots to take hold and have a better chance of thriving.

Also be aware of the vegetables that need to have as much sun as possible and those which require shade. Even though this is something that should be considered for any type of plant, it is especially important for vegetables. Certain vegetables like eggplants, peppers and tomatoes grow best in the sun while endive, arugula and Swiss chard grow best in the shade.

Chapter 5: How To Set Up Garden Irrigation

Irrigating the garden is limited to two main options, drip irrigation systems and sprinklers. Even though sprinklers can be further categorized into manual and automatic varieties, the function is the same.

Drip irrigation systems can be manual or automatic as well. Apart from these two options, manual watering can also be taken care of with the gardener in control of the hose, watering plants when required.

Whether or not a drip system or sprinklers are used, using the automated option makes the process that much easier. Many automated systems have sprinklers underground and the sprinklers come up at particular times (previously set by the gardener using a timer), and they water the garden and return underground when complete. This provides the necessary water for the garden without having to deal with unsightly sprinkler heads.

These sprinkler systems irrigate the garden by spraying the water in an upward motion so that it can fall back on the vegetables and soak into the soil. This also allows the leaves to be watered, which may be required if the plants thrive best in humid conditions but are planted in a dry area.

The main disadvantage of these systems is that a portion of the water will be lost in the process of evaporation no matter when the watering takes place.

Drip systems work well to provide adequate amounts of water to the root system decreasing the possibility of water evaporating. It is a much more efficient option to a sprinkler system. To the small gardener this may not be the major concern, but it is a major one for large farms.

Many of them use drip irrigation systems today. The pipes that are used can easily be concealed. The main disadvantage is that the leaves will not be watered, which may not be an issue if the particular plant does not require it.

Making use of a manual garden irrigation system is probably the most labor intensive and time- consuming option. A gardener has to spend a lot of time in the garden using watering hoses. Though this may not be the best approach for all gardeners, it does work well in particular circumstances, such as when the plants need varying amounts of water.

The selection of one of these systems comes down to personal preference and budget. The more expensive systems tend to be automatic drip systems and automatic sprinkler systems. Manual options are pretty affordable but have to be moved by the gardener as required. It is a bit inconvenient, but it is the better financial option.

Setting Up a Drip Irrigation System for Your Plants and Gardens

The process of drip irrigation provides water in drips, or at a very slow rate, to the roots of plants. It is a great way to conserve water as it enables water to travel to a deeper level than at the surface, which can cause waste due to runoff and evaporation.

When the lines for drip irrigation are installed, they do not have to be covered unless you want them to be. They can also easily be moved and adjusted as necessary.

Supplies for Drip Irrigation:

- Automatic timer – turns the drip action off and on
- Polyethylene tubing or hose (usually half an inch) – makes up the main lines of the system
- Anti-siphon control valve – stops the water used for irrigation water from getting into your home drinking water system
- Hose fitting and connectors – connects numerous lines of tubing
- Pressure regulator – keeps the water pressure coming from the faucet at about thirty psi (usually the suggested pressure for these systems)
- Polyethylene micro tubing – moves water from the main lines to the plants
- Filter – keeps debris from getting into the emitters and clogging them
- Emitters – these distribute water to the plants

These systems can be bought as individual parts or can be bought as kits.

When making plans for an irrigation system, all plants in the garden should be taken into consideration and a list should be made that describes their watering requirements.

If these areas are mapped out, you will have an easier time deciding where the lines ought to go and which lines need to provide more water than others. Some guidelines are outlined below:

- Large shrubs and trees – need occasional deep watering
- Flower/sun flower beds – needs lots of watering as they dry out faster than beds in the shade
- Vegetable gardens – need a lot of watering
- Shade beds – need occasional watering
- Hanging baskets and containers – needs frequent watering

Getting Started

If you are a newbie when it comes to drip irrigation, the perfect tool is the kit. When the kit is purchased, make sure that it is expandable so that new drip lines can be added when required.

You can also make use of the planning guides provided by the manufacturer to build your own system using individual parts like valves, emitters, fittings and tubing. The guides are usually product-specific and the instructions are outlined step by step.

Chapter 6: How To Keep Your Garden Pest Free

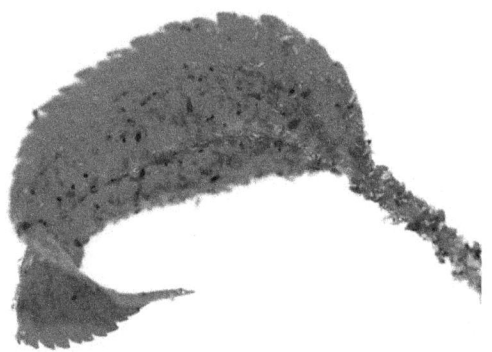

Pests can be annoying, and they can invade and destroy a garden. Though bugs will always be in gardens, harmful chemicals need not be used to get rid of them. There are a number of great organic solutions that can reduce or eliminate pests without leaving any harmful toxic residues that can get into groundwater. Some great options are outlined below.

Aphids, also known as plant lice, are extremely common and a number of species can be found on plants. They are small insects with soft bodies and needlelike mouths. They suck the sap out of plants while injecting their saliva, which is toxic to plants. The saliva causes the leaves and stems to become discolored. These aphids can be black, red, yellow, green or brown depending on the species, but they can be eradicated with the same methods. They are a bit difficult to handle – aphids are actually born pregnant and as a result, they multiply quickly.

To start the eradication process try growing plants that will attract praying mantis, lacewings and hoverflies, ladybugs (fennel, golden marguerite, Queen Anne's lace yarrows, dill) and parasitic wasps (cosmos, sunflowers, yarrow, hairy vetch, buckwheat, parsley, sweet alyssum). Plants that have strong scents also deter aphids - like mint, yarrow, catnip, basil and chives.

Snails and slugs are easy to spot because they leave a slimy trail. They can be found on greens like lettuce; they tend to come out at night and stay hidden in the daytime. There are several natural methods that can be used to control them. One great trick is to use eggshells. They have very soft bellies and will not go over crushed eggshells. Place them beneath the plants you want to protect. Another option is to use beer to make a trap – place a shallow dish or a funnel filled with beer on the ground close to the plants.

It is irresistible to slugs and they will crawl in and drown.

Though rabbits are cute, they are very nimble, sneaky and persistent when it comes to your vegetables. They are able to dig approximately two feet into the ground to get under a fence. The best defense you can mount is to use chicken wire. You will have to dig deep into the ground and put not only out the chicken wire into the ground but also above ground. You can also make an all-natural garlic spray that will keep them away.

Mosquitoes pose more danger to the gardener. No one wants to be bitten. The main ingredient in standard bug sprays is DEET, which has been linked to seizures, rashes, developmental and reproductive toxicity, and cancer. Thankfully there is a safer way to repel these annoying pests. Natural repellents that contain eucalyptol can be used. They are highly effective and non-toxic.

The caterpillar is an eating machine that can flatten a garden in no time. After they change into moths or butterflies, they become great allies, helping to keep the pest population down. Just like slugs or snails they have soft stomachs and will not go over crushed eggshells.

Caterpillars can easily be removed by hand and relocated to another part of the garden, or they can be eradicated using specific soaps or sprays.

The leafhopper is pretty hard to spot, but it does a lot of damage to plants. They are insects that suck sap, so the plants that they feed on tend to have leaves that have a burnt and crispy appearance at the ends.

To get rid of these pests, grow a little goldenrod, verbena, candytuft, yarrow, parsley, cilantro, dill, sweet alyssum or thyme to attract parasitic wasps, which are their natural enemy. Leafhoppers do not like geraniums, either.

The Colorado potato beetle is also known as the pill bug or potato bug. These beetles not only thrive on potatoes but will attack peppers, eggplants, tomatoes and other vegetables. To deter them, plant highly scented plants like garlic, catnip and yarrow.

All-Natural Repellents

There are occasions when a gardener will need to kick the level of pest control up a notch. The temptation to buy chemical pesticides should be avoided. Below are some easy recipes made from non-toxic items that can be used to help rid the garden of unwanted pests:

Insecticide Soap

This soap gets into the insects' skin causing dehydration and eventual extermination. It works well for insects with soft bodies. Start by mixing one to two tablespoons of soap with a quart of water. The soap should be a biodegradable and plant-based liquid soap. The mixture can then be poured into a spray bottle and used to spray pests as required. This can be used in addition to the others listed below to make it even more potent.

Pesticide Spray

Acquire some spices and roots with strong scents like rhubarb, mint, onions, garlic, ginger, horseradish and cayenne. Add enough water to cover them, then boil the mixture and leave the solution to soak overnight. Strain the solids from the liquid and dispose of the solids.

The liquid should then be poured into a spray bottle along with some of the soap solution. The spray will be good for several weeks. You can also make a variation using garlic. Instead of using the herbs outlined above, use 1 to 2 heads of garlic. Rabbits and deer do not like the scent.

Caffeine Spray

As humans we enjoy the energy boost we get from caffeine, but aphids and other insects do not. Caffeine spray is another creative and safe way to repel them. Mix artemisia, catnip, rue, lavender, thyme, pennyroyal, tansy or yarrow with 2 cups of water and 2 tablespoons of used coffee grounds. The mixture should sit for approximately 24 hours before it is strained and put into a spray bottle. The spray will last for several weeks.

Other Types of Pest Control

One of the most appropriate ways to keep your garden adequately protected is to grow healthy plants that do not have any disease in the first place. Plants that are sick are easy targets for pests, and they succumb to damage easily. Healthy plants are hardier. Take the time to inspect leaves regularly for any damage or discoloration. Deal with problems by removing an entire damaged plant, if needed, or by pinching off the dead parts.

Water plants based on their requirements and keep them from becoming malnourished by using organic compost and fertilizers. Managing weeds will also cut down on the possibility of pests.

A reminder – do not be afraid to put in plants that attract insects that are beneficial to your garden like spiders, ladybugs, praying mantis, lacewings, wasps and bees.

Chapter 7: What Crops To Plant In Your Garden

If you are planning to start a vegetable garden in the spring, the planning process can never be started too early. Get your hands on as many seeds catalogs as you can. They come with a lot of great photos and advice.

If you are a novice, think of starting with one (or all!) of the ten crops we will cover in this chapter. They are easy to grow and they provide ample menu options. A few of the crops work best from seedlings, but most can be grown from seeds.

Radishes can be planted in the fall and spring and will do well in soil that is not so great. Your first will be ready in a few weeks.

Spring Planting

Salad greens refer to corn, arugula, spinach, and lettuce. You can pick your favorite or grow a mix. A lot of companies will sell mixed packets for winter and summer gardening. The seeds can be planted in the fall and spring and can be harvested year round.

Green beans are easy to grow. You can freeze what you cannot use right away. The seeds need to be planted after the spring frost is gone. (Not before!)

Onions are great with any meal. You can start with small plants and harvest the bulbs when they are ready, or just eat the greens if you like.

Strawberries are hardy plants and thrive in a sunny spot. Wait until spring to plant them.

Bell peppers and hot peppers are easy to grow. You can start with plants and pick the peppers at varying stages of maturity to get a variety in flavors and colors.

Zucchini is from the squash family and will not take up much garden space. It can be grown from transplants or seeds and is very prolific. A few plants can produce a bumper crop.

Nothing tastes better than a nice ripe tomato. Start with some plants and wait for the harvest. Any excess tomatoes can be frozen or canned.

Many herbs will grow without a lot of care. Basil is one of them. It can easily be grown from transplants and seeds.

The easiest way to grow potatoes is to grow them in straw as opposed to soil. Cut sections of potatoes referred to as seeds can be bought in early spring.

Crops for Fall

Your garden will produce much better crops if you plant "green manure" in the fall. "Green manure" is otherwise known as a cover crop and it works hard in your garden. You may think that these crops are only for large growers or for farmland, but a small backyard garden can receive the same benefits.

One of the major benefits of cover crops is that they will improve soil quality when the garden is not being used. Cover crops also keep weeds at bay, control disease and pests, prevent soil erosion, promote organic production of nitrogen, and provide organic matter. Cover crops also repair the soil. They control the level of micronutrients and macronutrients, as well as giving gardens a more pleasing look and a pop of color in the winter months.

The best crops for the Fall are buckwheat, sorghum, millet and Sudan grass as well as legumes like velvet beans, sesbania, vetch, annual sweet clover, soybeans and cow peas. Legumes provide nitrogen for the soil while the other crops help to add biomass to the soil and keep the weeds away.

For the Novice Gardener, the Easier Cover Crops to Grow Are:

Cereal Rye: two varieties can be found - cereal rye and annual rye. Cereal rye should be planted at the start of the Fall season and will keep growing until late Fall, then start growing again in Spring. It tolerates cold temperatures well.

Annual rye allows you to plant your garden earlier. The crop does not have to be turned into the soil at springtime.

Field Peas are a wonderful mix of grain and legumes that can withstand cold temperatures and provide the soil with nitrogen.

Oats are a great provider of organic matter.

Buckwheat grows rather quickly and serves as a canopy for weeds. The key is not to let it go to seed if you want some buckwheat to harvest.

Clover can be found in many sizes and shapes. It fixes nitrogen and makes the soil richer. Yellow sweet clover especially helps build good soil structure and is an excellent soil amender. Crimson clover works just as well.

If you have decided to plant these cover crops, ensure that they have enough time to take root. This means planting them at least four weeks before the killing frost.

All you have to do is rake the garden soil gently. Spread the seeds and rake them into the soil, then water, especially if your location does not get much rain.

The major thing to keep in mind is that the crops need to be destroyed before they set seed. Cover crops are only grown for a specific period of time and need to be plowed before they get to full maturity to improve the soil quality.

The ideal time to do this is when the seeds start to show on grains or the plants start to flower. Annuals can be killed simply by cutting the base and waiting for 48 hours for the stems and leaves to dry, and then digging them in and wait for them to decompose. Planting of flowers or vegetables can begin three weeks later.

Crop Rotation

One of the rules governing good garden practices is to rotate plant families each season The main reason for crop rotation is to maintain the balance of microorganisms, organic matter, and nutrients. The micro-creatures that live in the soil are the ones that benefit the most from this process.

Let us use potatoes for an example of the importance of rotation. During a season, the fungus that gives the skin scabby patches may multiply, along with verticillium fungus, which kills roots and damages eggplants and tomatoes as well as small nematodes that damage potatoes. Should the potatoes be replanted in the same area, the crop will fail.

Planting them in another section will prevent these issues. Bear in mind that what affects one crop will not necessarily affect another.

Field tests show that yield will fall by approximately 40% as a result of disease from lack of crop rotation. Apart from breaking the cycle of disease, the rotation of crops can cut down on the loss of nutrients. In the same way that beets and beans need manganese, tomatoes need calcium. Crop needs vary.

Planning Rotation

Draw a rough sketch of the garden, making note of the row(s) and bed sizes. Jot down the locations of the last set of crops. Taking photos of your garden year to year can help you keep records.

Another piece of paper can be cut to fit the beds or rows that you have in your first drawing. Make some crop markers by writing down the crop and the family they belong to. I would advise to have a few beds available for experimenting.

Move the markers around until you accomplish good rotation. Getting it perfect will take a number of seasons - the aim is to get the crops rotated in a particular direction and in a particular order. It can be circular, front to back, or left to right. Creativity is necessary.

Family Rotation: The Nine Main Groups

When crops are sorted into families, the process of rotation is much easier. The major families of plants are:

- Carrot family: parsnips, parsley, celery and carrots
- Onion family: shallots, leeks, garlic and onions
- Cabbage family: kohlrabi, rutabagas, leafy greens, kale, Brussels sprouts, broccoli and cabbage
- Sunflower family: sunflowers, lettuce, and other leafy greens
- Spinach family: chard and beets
- Pea family: beans and peas
- Cucumber family: gourds, squash, melons and cucumbers
- Tomato family: rye, oats, wheat and corn

Go forth and eat what you grow from your garden!

MEET THE AUTHOR

For years William Whittaker toyed with the idea of becoming more self-sufficient in providing food for his family. While living close to an Amish community, he had the opportunity to see how they lived and how they worked and lived off the land by growing their own livestock and crops and using a barter system to get items they did not produce on their own.

With his wife, he decided to start with a small backyard garden, growing a few essential vegetables like tomatoes, cabbage, lettuce, and some herbs. As they became more experienced, their garden expanded. He now regularly shares his bounty with his neighbors and extended family members.

www.ingramcontent.com/pod-product-compliance
Ingram Content Group UK Ltd.
Pitfield, Milton Keynes, MK11 3LW, UK
UKHW022119230426
12048UKWH00010BA/607